TURNING POINTS IN U.S. HISTORY
INDUSTRIAL REVOLUTION

by Veronica B. Wilkins

pogo

Ideas for Parents and Teachers

Pogo Books let children practice reading informational text while introducing them to nonfiction features such as headings, labels, sidebars, maps, and diagrams, as well as a table of contents, glossary, and index.

Carefully leveled text with a strong photo match offers early fluent readers the support they need to succeed.

Before Reading

- "Walk" through the book and point out the various nonfiction features. Ask the student what purpose each feature serves.
- Look at the glossary together. Read and discuss the words.

Read the Book

- Have the child read the book independently.
- Invite him or her to list questions that arise from reading.

After Reading

- Discuss the child's questions. Talk about how he or she might find answers to those questions.
- Prompt the child to think more. Ask: Many inventions were created during the Industrial Revolution. What do you use that was created during this time?

Pogo Books are published by Jump!
5357 Penn Avenue South
Minneapolis, MN 55419
www.jumplibrary.com

Library of Congress Cataloging-in-Publication Data

Names: Wilkins, Veronica B., 1994– author.
Title: Industrial revolution / Veronica B. Wilkins.
Description: Minneapolis, MN: Jump!, Inc., [2020]
Series: Turning points in U.S. history
Audience: Age: 7–10. | Includes index.
Identifiers: LCCN 2019020740 (print)
LCCN 2019021896 (ebook)
ISBN 9781645271437 (ebook)
ISBN 9781645271413 (hardcover : alk. paper)
ISBN 9781645271420 (pbk. : alk. paper)
Subjects: LCSH: Industrial revolution–United States
Juvenile literature.
Classification: LCC HC105 (ebook)
LCC HC105 .W535 2020 (print)
DDC 330.973/05–dc23
LC record available at https://lccn.loc.gov/2019020740

Editor: Susanne Bushman
Designer: Jenna Casura

Photo Credits: Pictorial Press Ltd/Alamy, cover; Hulton Archive/Getty, 1, 16; Everett Historical/Shutterstock, 3; De Agostini Picture Library/Age Fotostock, 4; Detroit Publishing Co./Library of Congress, 5; National Photo Company Collection/Library of Congress, 6-7; connerscott1/iStock, 8; karelnoppe/Shutterstock, 9 (background); Bettmann/Getty, 9 (image on tablet), 18-19 (foreground); GL Archive/Alamy, 10-11; Everett Collection Historical/Alamy, 12-13; John C. H. Grabill Collection/Library of Congress, 14-15; Lewis Wickes Hine/National Child Labor Committee Collection/Library of Congress, 17; ADragan/Shutterstock, 18-19 (background); imtmphoto/Shutterstock, 20-21; Science & Society Picture Library/Getty, 23.

Printed in the United States of America at Corporate Graphics in North Mankato, Minnesota.

TABLE OF CONTENTS

early version of Alexander Graham Bell's telephone

CHAPTER 1

CHANGING TIMES

In the early 1800s, the steamboat was a new **invention**. Steam **engines** powered these boats. Before this, humans powered boats. They used paddles, oars, or sails. Steam engines made **transportation** faster.

steamboat

Soon, steamboats moved many people and goods. They were one of many inventions during the **Industrial Revolution**.

The Industrial Revolution started in England around 1760. It spread to America around 1790. It lasted about 150 years.

What was life like before this? Most people lived on farms. They grew their own food. They made goods by hand. Humans and horses ran farming tools. Towns were small and far apart.

CHAPTER 2
INVENTIONS AND FACTORIES

Samuel Slater opened a **textile mill** on the East Coast in 1793. It was the first of many U.S. **factories**. More factory machines were invented. They made work easier and faster. Workers used them to make products.

Samuel Slater's textile mill

Textile mills wove cotton into fabric. In 1793, Eli Whitney invented the cotton gin. It cleaned picked cotton. It was faster than human workers.

cotton gin ·····▶

Whitneyville

Whitney changed how factories worked. How? He began making products with interchangeable parts around 1800. These parts were the same. They could be used in any of the same product. Now, products could be **mass produced**.

Whitney created a town around his factory. It was called Whitneyville. Many companies did this. Workers lived in homes the companies owned. They shopped at company stores.

Factories made exciting new products. Radios, telephones, and cars were just a few. These products made **communication** and travel faster and easier.

Assembly lines helped make products faster. Henry Ford used them to make cars starting in 1913. Assembly lines still make products today.

DID YOU KNOW?

Before the assembly line, it took more than 12 hours to make a car frame. With an assembly line, it took just one and a half hours!

Ford assembly line

car frame

Workers finished train tracks across the country in 1869. Steam engine trains traveled between the West and East Coasts. They carried mail, food, factory products, and even people.

DID YOU KNOW?

Trains took people across the country in just four days. Before trains, people traveled by horse or wagon. This trip took months!

CHAPTER 3

CITIES GROW

By the 1870s, U.S. cities were full of factories. Farmers moved to cities to work in them. Cities grew quickly. This helped factories. But it caused some problems, too. Cities became crowded and dirty.

Kids worked in factories. Why? The money they made helped support their families. Factory work was dangerous. There were few safety laws. Kids were often hurt. They worked long hours. They were paid little.

strike

Our Share?

More School Less Hospita

WE ARE protected by a tariff

WE ask for stice

WE Want to Go to School

Nothin

Adult workers were also treated poorly. Workers formed **unions**. They also planned **strikes**. Why? They hoped these would force **employers** to pay them more and create better working conditions.

TAKE A LOOK!

Not many people lived in cities in the early 1800s.
See how the Industrial Revolution changed that.

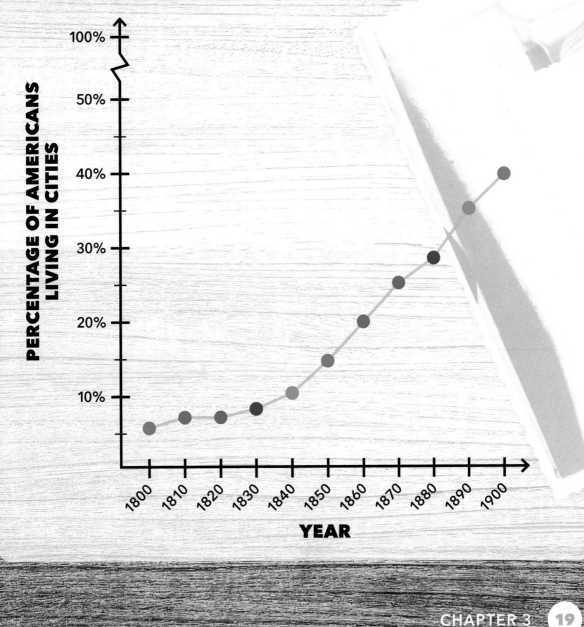

The Industrial Revolution changed a lot about U.S. life. Cities grew. Laws began protecting workers. Inventions and factories made things easier. Inventions from this time still help us today!

WHAT DO YOU THINK?

The Industrial Revolution made daily life easier. Do you use phones, cars, or light bulbs? These were invented during this time. What would you like to invent? How would it make life easier?

QUICK FACTS & TOOLS

TIMELINE

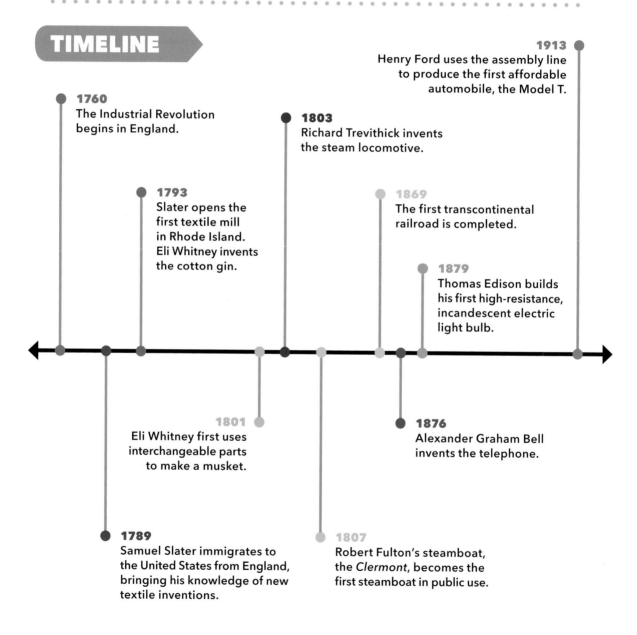

1913
Henry Ford uses the assembly line to produce the first affordable automobile, the Model T.

1760
The Industrial Revolution begins in England.

1803
Richard Trevithick invents the steam locomotive.

1793
Slater opens the first textile mill in Rhode Island. Eli Whitney invents the cotton gin.

1869
The first transcontinental railroad is completed.

1879
Thomas Edison builds his first high-resistance, incandescent electric light bulb.

1801
Eli Whitney first uses interchangeable parts to make a musket.

1876
Alexander Graham Bell invents the telephone.

1789
Samuel Slater immigrates to the United States from England, bringing his knowledge of new textile inventions.

1807
Robert Fulton's steamboat, the *Clermont*, becomes the first steamboat in public use.

GLOSSARY

assembly lines: Arrangements of machines in factories through which products pass from one person or machine to the next, with each performing a small, separate task.

communication: The activity of sharing information, ideas, or feelings.

employers: People or companies that provide jobs and pay wages to workers.

engines: Machines that make things move.

factories: Buildings where products are made in large numbers using machines.

Industrial Revolution: The rapid and major change in economy in the United States and England from roughly 1760 to 1920. This era is marked by the introduction of power-driven machinery and urbanization.

invention: A useful product that is created through study and experiment.

mass produced: Made in large, identical amounts with machines in a factory.

strikes: Situations in which workers refuse to work until their demands are met.

textile mill: A factory in which different types of fabric or fibers, such as yarn, are produced and processed into usable products.

transportation: A way to travel from one place to another.

unions: Organized groups of workers set up to help improve working conditions.

Thomas Edison's light bulb

TO LEARN MORE

Finding more information is as easy as 1, 2, 3.

❶ Go to www.factsurfer.com

❷ Enter "IndustrialRevolution" into the search box.

❸ Choose your book to see a list of websites.

FACT SURFER